Praise for THE VELOCITY (

Kathryn Gahl addresses her grandson from embryo to the eternal in poems that chronicle what their lives might have been together: boisterous, joyous discovery, voluminous love and snuggling. Spoken directly to the child, these poems are both beautiful and terrible. No woman, grandmother, mother should feel the need to write these, but there is the power of poetry, its ability to say the unsayable. "Everywhere / I feel you: my head wobbly, / ribs imprisoned, heart seizing / at the thought of you /...." These poems will break your heart.

KARLA HUSTON, Wisconsin Poet Laureate 2017–2018

Kathryn Gahl's *The Velocity of Love* is a rollercoaster read – the slow rise with a gorgeous view, the foreboding pause at the top, and then the unbearable plummet. These poems are both ethereal and meaty, beautiful renderings of a terrible experience. A genuine wow.

CATHRYN COFELL, author of *Stick Figure With Skirt*

The Velocity of Love is a balm in Gilead which Kathryn Gahl delivers in a concise language of everyday life. Gahl unflinchingly carries us with her through a crucible of loss, which ultimately reveals itself to be a pathway of love—a love which forges a universalizing wholeness of being. Gahl invites the reader in with "the small of me in the arc of you," and "Be beautiful. / Be fierce. / Be anything but mad." With a clarity of vision, such as "how we hold our / head to joy / because we have seen / another side," Gahl shows us how to "favor circles over straight lines" and embrace life's gifts—"such a fine beat / I shall dance to it."

SYLVIA CAVANAUGH, author of *Icarus: An Anthropology of Addiction*

Kathryn Gahl is a poet, who with the simplest quotidian essentials, makes poems like tiny tornados. They could whoop up the leaves under a shedding tree in spring or autumn and highlight the simultaneous life and death of their bittersweet movement. In her touching collection, *The Velocity of Love*, the anticipation, appreciation, and lamentation of the grandchild before his arrival, during his brief stay on earth, and after his death are explored tenderly and arched with a radical optimism and radical love. Sweet and sour are as balanced in these moving poems that in their form, grief, and pleasure lend homage to William Carlos Williams. Come, celebrate life's full cycle at the velocity of love.

MAYA MARSHALL, author of *All The Blood Involved in Love*

Gahl's poems reveal a life lived with a generous, unguarded heart that leaves her open to the full range between immense joy and great despair. The poems, arranged in three sections, encompass her grandson's gestation, arrival, growth and the grief around his death. From cosmos to crayons, thistles to fields of sweet clover, roots and wings, genomes and nuclear rods to the perfect sticky peach Gahl always achieves the honest balance between life's ongoing realities and incredible miracles. Gahl encourages us to "Be beautiful, be fierce, be anything but mad." *The Velocity of Love* leaves it clear that the universe is full of mystery with no obligation for explanations. Her poems and love notes reveal Gahl's journey toward peace.

JENNA RINDO, *Wisconsin People & Ideas* Poetry Winner 2018

Kathryn Gahl's latest collection, *The Velocity of Love*, chronicles the unconditional love of a grandmother. In poems ranging from whimsical to philosophical, Gahl's voice reflects the dreams and realities across generations. The collection is an insightful meditation, grounded in natural details—celestial bodies, blossoms, the accoutrements of childhood, a simple breakfast. The poetic range is stitched together with Gahl's gift for detail and nuance, "a chance to communicate / about a long life-line and / how short it is, really." Playing with sound and form, these spare poems remind us life happens in juxtaposition—joy and sorrow, life and death—and "it is in wavering that / we learn to find balance." In "This, I Believe, Is What You Are Telling Me," Gahl focuses on specific tasks to help survive the loss. *The Velocity of Love* resonates with the business of living, loving, dying, and grieving, tasks that unite us all.

JESSICA VAN SLOOTEN, Associate Professor, English, Writing, Women's & Gender Studies, UW-GB

A brave love song for a child too early lost. Prepare for a roller coaster range of emotions. And witness the love. Always the love.

JULIA DAVIS, Director, Kiel Public Library

Kathryn Gahl's *The Velocity of Love* is a compelling and heart-rending collection of tiny stories in the shape of poems—stories in which "gaiety tumbles from heaven, and "People / betray one / another," where "so much depended / upon / a baby carriage," and we wake every day "with a fresh case of missing." These spare, delicate poems evoke the everydayness of life while reminding us of the joy, wonder, and unspeakable sorrow of that life.

PETER GILBERT, Director, Seeley G. Mudd Library, Lawrence University

In these poems, Kathryn Gahl anticipates, celebrates, and commemorates a life, a very brief life, but one which nevertheless reverberates far beyond the reckoning of birthdays and calendars. The poems are intimate, rich with imagery, and though quite personal, wrestle with a very ancient and ongoing, and necessary human task—how to find words for joys and losses beyond words, or as one of the poems eloquently puts it, how "to let in dark/ and bend it light."

MAX GARLAND, Wisconsin Poet Laureate 2013-2014

In *The Velocity of Love*, Kathryn Gahl takes the unimaginable and gives it a form. Many forms. From the joyful announcement of new life like a snowflake on an upturned face—the ultimate of unique—to the reality of an empty baby carriage, this is the story of a life that came and went too soon. These succinct, crystalline poems have the power to lift you, shake you, drop you, and lift you again. Once you have *The Velocity of Love* in your heart, you will not think about life—or death—in the same way ever again.

LISA VIHOS, Poetry and Arts Editor, *Stoneboat Literary Journal*

In *The Velocity of Love*, Kathryn Gahl writes for, about, and in celebration of her grandson. With each poem "a pearl, a pulse / felt and heard," the poet moves from joyful anticipation into the full flowering of love. In the last section, she teaches us all love is paired with grief, whether we're prepared for it or not. With taut control and craft, the "barb and thistle of life" bristles and dances in these lines, supple and surprising, devastating and tenacious.

SARAH SADIE, author of *We Are Traveling Through Dark at Tremendous Speed*

The Velocity of Love

THE VELOCITY OF LOVE

KATHRYN GAHL

Water's Edge Press

For information, contact the publisher.

Printed in the United States of America

Water's Edge Press LLC
Sheboygan, WI
watersedgepress.com

ISBN: 978-1-952526-00-8
Library of Congress Control Number: 2020938593

Credits

"Morning" appeared in *Intersections: Art and Poetry*, Sheboygan Visual Artists and Mead Public Library Poetry Circle, 2016.
"Because of That Cherry Chocolate Cake, Here is Advice for My Grandson," appeared in *The Summerset Review*, 2013.
"How To Be Happy" appeared in *Wisconsin Fellowship of Poets' Calendar*, 2014.

Cover image artwork copyright Jamie Heiden 2020
Author photo by Owen Zylstra

A WATER'S EDGE PRESS FIRST EDITION

FOR LEO

It is not how long a star shines
but the brightness of its light

Contents

Anticipation

Realization

Lamentation

Anticipation

At Whistling Straits

We gather
with skies eggshell blue
and grass spring green
to celebrate several birthdays
or so I think

when my daughter's sunny
voice beams the news
of your upcoming
wintery birth—her first.

Suddenly,
gaiety tumbles from heaven
        a wisp of winter
        glorious joy snow
and a single
delicate crystal
seems to land on my cheek
        innocent and rare
        the ultimate in unique

Her Room

Will you
come to magnify

the moon, the stars,
        the iris
of purple fervor
given by your father
to your mother

gracing her room
        dreamily
        abloom
reflecting the cosmos
the crayons to come

Nighttime

      Listen, little grey fish
swimming in your mother's
warm water pool
      drifting in
      from infinity
a floating lotus
a tiny light spinning
in the night sky

      Listen, I say to you,
though what I mean is
it is I
who will listen
and wait
under the arch of heaven

until I hear you.

And then
one night
      in my dreams

I swear, I already do

Beautiful and Terrible

what is it with water
a bag of amniotic fluid
in your mother

her undulating lines
running like a river
lazy or rampant

breast stroke, breast milk
springing forth
an eternal source

unknown and wet
molecules terribly beautiful
growing

around a pearl, a pulse
felt and heard

The Physical World Meets the Virtual

Take one water lily,
a yellow canary, and
a white rabbit.

Add the rustle of leaves.
Stir in a few
scampering stars.

This will be your originality.

Already, I see it.
Believe it.

I know you
do
too.

Music for the Unborn Child

I bought you
a CD and played
it in the car

Actually it is for
your mama

to tap a musical
beat on her belly
and watch you respond, kicking
in the same rhythm
        Da-da dum, da-da-dum

Well, when I went to remove
the disc
from the Subaru CD player,
it got stuck.

Sounds about right.
I'm stuck on you.

Baby Bump Week Nine—Size of an Olive

The olive green
and verdant
soft with calling
a garnishment
a promise
a salty idea
saucy as a rising moon
and even
mama's mood
when choosing
a crib
for you
little olive

Field

your parents
have been through the
barb and thistle of life

and today's
ingenious ultrasound
shows them and me

your picture-perfect body
head bobbing like a bluebird
in a field of sweet clover

and between your legs
a divining rod
in motion

in search of
hidden wisdom
the future called hope

Stars and Stripes

Today our
nation celebrates
Memorial Day

honoring those
who went and killed

and I trust
you are coming
not for the killing

but for
the curing

Where You Came From

Not from war
time like your grand
papa arriving full of
the feud
and his job it turned out
to keep it going

Not of peace
time like your grand
mama arriving while
India starved and
her job to study what
satisfied

But of ardent desire
        your parents
old enough to know
a raspberry bush
does not yield the first season
after planting

yet when it does
a bounty
of lovable pleasure

.

One Long and Two Short

When I was
growing up
at the end
(it could have been the beginning)
of a half-mile gravel drive

a black phone
hung on the wall. It sported
a short furry cord
and a hand-held
receiver to snug around my ear.

Someday, I hope you will
ask me what one long and
two short has to do with
a phone in a farmhouse
kitchen—it will give us
a chance to communicate
about a long life-line and
how short it is, really.

What Used to be Part of a Parking Lot

is now an outdoor bistro
where your mother, uncle,
and I sit with Veda
a soft-coated wheaten terrier

after completing
our yearly visit to the grave
of a man gone twelve years

a man my children called Papa
a man you can still call Opa

because if a parking lot
can be a bistro
then a man
can be more than a memory

Tomato, Tomato

This week you have
grown to tomato size
and not just any tomato

an heirloom tomato
with all the resonant
complex genes that make

a tomato hit every
sense: sight touch
taste smell and

even hearing
the sizzle of steak
on Daddy's grill

while Mama cradles
your genome, all that came
before to make you. You.

Feast

Get ready
for a lifetime
of good eating

because
your mother
knows how to

cook, her apron of care
handed down
from my mother's
kitchen to mine
to hers

along with
savory tastes, too

After the Announcement is Made

First one uncle
then another
first one aunt
then another
     exclaim
          marvel
               gleam

clapping hands with
cousins crazy with happy

when they hear
of your coming.

And from then on
saxophones and soft drums

velvet tongues
voicing
aaw-aww-aaaw

In other words:
Awe

Sun Ball

The ball bouncing
with a catchy rhythm
the first time your Mama
            heard your heartbeat

not the first time
she cries hot tears
            cold tears

yet this the first
audible note that you are
            here
you are OhMyGod
            here
            here
alive and jumping for joy.

Such a fine beat
I shall dance to it

Toys

By now there exist
more toys than
anyone's days on earth

many of them
plastic inventions
of greedy minds.

I hope you will
crawl inside your
own mind—

bang spoons on kettles
pound pots with paddles
pretend piano on pans

and find new
harmonies, accord

Playtime

The woman down the street
has no children
(It is too late).

And so, she buys a dollhouse,
carpets it, wallpapers the
walls, installs beds and chairs
in an extravagant house (this, her second),
then adds teeny tiny replicas of vintage LIFE magazines,
a high chair, desk, sewing machine, and

other items needed to pretend
while I watch her

grateful for your coming.

This Week, You Size in as a Sweet Potato

oh sweet potato
sweet

you are all that
and more—

my sweet pea,
honeybun, my sugar

my morning
glory and cute petunia

my carrot seed
and soon bold oak

you are my nature
and I shall be your nurture

About that Sweet

I hesitate to tell you
this, now that
you have grown

to be
our sweet potato sweet

but you may as well know:
for the first time
in the 160-year history
of the Wisconsin State Fair

one can buy deep-fried
bacon-wrapped sweet
potato tots
on a stick

And I wonder:
does this interest you?

H is for Hat

and C is for cap

and
whichever one

you place on
your head

it will crown you
The King

with full reign
of my
open-hearted lands

Charge Cards

A lot of stuff
stuffs Mother Earth
around her outer rim

At times
I question how she
can spin without
falling off her axis
but maybe
she will pick up speed
to launch
the crap into outer space

and make room
for
the rich life

you will bring

Always Something

this week it's the
plum blue Subaru
threatening to blow a gasket

with an axle
leaking from its front strut

there are thunderstorm warnings
and tornadoes
and elsewhere tsunamis
mass gun shootings
earthquakes
nowhere to put
          spent nuclear rods
roads of cement crumbling
while the emerald ash borer
is sighted in Green Bay

lust and love collide
while I wait to keep you safe

Dear Baby

Dear Baby,
Your
parents
are fighting.

Dear Baby,
Where is your
place
in the family
story line?

Dear baby,
their baby.

Dear baby,
my baby.

Dear baby,
our baby.

Of Comparison

Fathers
made of broken parts,
motorcycles, barren nights

come from youth split
down the middle
like an angry sky

but fathers

also know how to fix
things, refashion a life
from pieces

and with mothers
will make
a masterpiece

this time
that being—you.

Complaint Department

Your mother has taken
to worrying

troublesome thoughts
about a crib, stroller,
the high cost of diapers,
car seats, a high chair

how long each day
she will leave you
at day care

to work to pay
        for day care, a mortgage, car loan,
        a pack of student debt
        on her back

when all she wants
is to stay home

with you—
be a mama, be happy

This Week, You Size in as a Cantaloupe

so quickly
a cantaloupe spills
from the vine

paints the palate
bright as a ball of sunshine

Having Seen Many Births

When you will arrive
wrinkled and full of
stork bites, crinkled
  as parchment paper
a drying rose, or even
edges of

a shirt after
someone takes a nap
and awakens

refreshed
raring to go—

I will be raring to go

With
you

There's a Chance

There's a
chance
you will turn
out to be

a high hugger
cuddler
or squeeze machine

Whichever one
you are
I will hold you
both near and afar

Moving Through Time and Space

Your step-grandpa works
        as a hospice doctor

and notices the
        biggest challenge

people face when
        leaving this world

is
fear.

I wonder
        if the same is true

about arriving
        and . . .

are you afraid

Some Kind of Perfect

One day
somewhere
someone will phone you
out of the blue
and say
  Hey
  Do you want to meet up

And I hope you do
I hope you
take a gamble

because there are
many
who will want
to meet you

Roots

Roots of the lupine
have grown through holes
in the little plastic box
I brought home
from the greenhouse

Gently,
I tap the box until
the plant loosens
its grip

and willing roots
leave
their small world

and slide
into my eager
warm palms

The Arrival

When you arrive
be very
aware of the small

space on your
back
between your shoulder blades.

Those are your wings.

Open them.

Realization

Boy Story

It will be about wheels.

Wheels to sit on, swing from,
pump, push, and ride.

Wheels to turn, burn,
race, and roll.

Wheels to make you
go 'round and 'round
which is fine

as long as you
come back
to me.

Mother

Your mother is weary, great
with love, lips full. And
her breasts pink at your cry.

Entrance

You came

with your toe in the sand
the sun in your eye
the juice of a peach.

You (and I) came from clouds
and the trees and leaves

you giggle at
as if they're alive
as if they sing to you

when you contemplate
their underside
of tiny veins
soaking up sun.

One day I will teach you
about photosynthesis.

I will teach you to take a photo
and synthesize it with music,

convert sunlight into sustenance
a process a million years old.

And we are an itty-bitty part of it.

Feet

So much
to love about your feet

how one day you
will decide to walk

on them and they
will hold, give you

balance and speed,
laugh when tickled.

They will spring you to the hoop,
push you through the pool

ankles, toes, and soles
dancing through every change.

What I Know and What I Want to Know

That you are here.
That it is now.
That you will outlive me.

That you will carry on
that you will cry on
and be okay when I am gone.

That you will remember
everything I taught you
the things we talked about
and the things we never got
around to, which you must imagine

when the neck of time snaps
and paralyzes me
like your great grandmother.

And always we shall remember
when you learned to walk
how you lifted your butt,
the foot, the heel

and felt the shift to the other hip—
the possibility
you inherited my walk.

Sailing

The day
we
set sail

the wind
will lift
us

and we will
brown like
two cookies

in a sun oven
baking the day
delicious

How To Be Happy

Do not compare yourself to those
around you.
Eat a perfect soft-boiled egg.
Wear a baseball cap backwards.
Learn a skill. Snuggle.
Keep a window open year-round.
Lose with grace.
Be kind—others will be kinder to you.
Giggle.
Become aware of breath—yours first,
  then, others.
People who hold their breath will
      try to steal yours. Share it.

When I Hear You Crying in the Night

your wailing finds
us together
with our ancestors

who each in their time
answered the call
whether alert or sleepy

grappling with flesh
with a miracle

extending arms and palms

opening up
when someone
expects it

Because Of That Cherry Chocolate Cake,
    Here Is Advice For My Grandson

I bought one
big fat slice
of cake yesterday
at Siebkens
for your grandpa

and when I got
home
I ate half of it.

Today I must admit
I ate
the other half.

People
betray one
another.

I thought you should know.

Table in the Store

a tiny table
stands on four
legs shaped like #2 pencils

each leg painted
canary yellow with a
honey of an eraser at the tip

and did I mention
the table top
is red   apple red   cherry red

it is so eye-popping red
it makes me
fast-forward

to when   you will sit
at it

and color—
outside the lines
of course

Thunderstorms Today

shattering balls
            of rain
                        hit the roof
and your mother
            weeps in
                        her bed
worrying
            over how she
                        will keep you
from
            her own
                        storms

Graduation Speech

There are only two
important days
in a life

the speaker said.

One is the day you are born.
The other is the day you

figure out
why
you are here.

About that Graduation Speech

I am not the
graduation speaker

I am the Oma
who was there
the day you were born

and I will be there
the day you graduate

because I trust
the long view

I trust in you

The Depressives

Some folks
open to the sound
of a doorbell
with hope

While others
hear
the knob turn
with trepidation
and ready themselves
for something
coming through the door
when in fact

it's already
  in the house

Hippie

there's a story
told about your
dead opa

how he walked
in the snow
wearing sandals

a free spirit
to be sure
who thirteen years

before you were born
broke free
of earth's gravity

his illusions
still out there

The Tricycle

the tricycle
rings
true
and
blue

it
is
waiting
for
you

The Global Village

In every hill
a stone

in every stone
a design

in every design
a line

in every line
a connection

in every connection
a curve

around every curve
an expectation

Us

The True Story of God

When your mama
was three and one-half
I asked her if
she believed in God.

She went into
slow-motion,
puzzled, a pause
before saying

I believe
in Owen
(her brother).

You are not
even close to
three
and one-half.

Nonetheless,
I believe in you.

Of Tired

Sleep now, my little one
Sleep and dream and stretch

Sleep now, my little one
Sleep and roll and yawn

Sleep now, my little one
Sleep and glide and fly

Sleep now, my little one
The waking world can wait

Lucky

If you are lucky
which you are

you will one day
walk a long
country lane
with a springy
dog on a
cooling summer eve
and the smell
of sun on gravel
will fill you

Thunder

Call it
rolling
rumbling
tumbling

the way a little boy
bursts on the scene
to throw me
a kiss that miraculously

I catch—I've never been
great with a bat
and a ball

but for my little boy
I can do anything

A Reason Everyone Needs a Dog

a reason
everyone needs a dog

requires
not a reason
but that season

following a barren
winter or a spring insane,
a hot muggy summer
or an autumn overdue

because a dog
will walk into your season
and never demand a reason
for loving you

Timepieces

there are clocks
you must learn to read
in this culture

and when you
learn what numbers
mean, be forewarned:

you come from
a line of people
who cannot

tell time
who are chronically late

forever lost in the now
loving each moment

with little worry
for what's next

The Admission

your mother
realizes
that she will
be fifty-three
when she
is dealing
with teenage angst
though I
don't think you
will be given
to teenage trouble
or waves of angst
but rather ripples
of goals, composed

The Liminal Place

there is such a place
my wee little sprite

it is the place
you
came from
with
a Delft blue bowl
on the kitchen table

and outside
a Monarch
who follows the bee
savoring the milkweed

urging you
to cross
the threshold

sit
here
with me

Dump Truck

Today I watch you play
and see you
driving truck
on a summer job
hauling
        sand
        and
        gravel
building roads

making
        the
        old
        new
by changing
the landscape
        of
        my
        life

The Unexplained

Humans make many things
they think are magical.
Crop-dusters
Spandex, Sonar, saxophones
and whoa, even
Apple watches and eerie Alexa.

But books,
according to Alice Hoffman,
may well be
the only
true magic.

Clearly, she never met you.

In the Afternoon

We lie on the living room carpet
side by side
beneath a double-hung window

staring at an oak tree
when the underside
of leaves catch

a spring breeze
symphonies of silvery
subdued light

the marvel
on your face

as you watch
like a choreographer
studying shadow and shape

or a balloonist
learning waft and lift

the heady sense
of movement, of miracle

Obligation

I'll tell you right now
someone will push you
to buy high-end jeans,

remote-control cars, talking
toys, humongous water pistols,
paint ball guns, or fatty fast food.

You are under
no obligation to buy any of it.

Your obligation
is simple—
amplify love.

Rattle

You have been awarded
a single lifetime
a limited span to

find your funny bone
and shake hands
with humanity.

So even though
you do not have your
first rattle in hand,

soon as you do—
hurry up, go!

Lamentation

Casket

When the undertakers
lowered your casket
into the earth

I dropped to the frozen ground
and curved into child's pose:
hips bent, feet under my butt,
arms stretched forward

a yoga pose so named because
it recreates the repose of a sleeping infant.

I stayed there a long time.

When the gravediggers came
with their shovels of dirt,
I stayed, kept watch.

To this day
I do not remember rising.
To this day I keep watch,
on guard.

The Baby Carriage

so much depended
upon

a baby carriage
waiting

next to the
the bassinet

next to the
rocking chair

next to the
picture books

next to the
fuzzy blanket

on the lap
ready to snuggle

This Part I Do Remember

After getting through the funeral

>   my son and I slid into the back
>   seat of a car

trusting the driver
to deliver us
to our destination.

>   But the driver
seemed to take one
sharp turn after another and
whether he did or not
veer from side to side
is not the point

since our heads whirled
our stomachs pitched
as we seemed to swerve
  like in a ride at the State Fair
except our screaming
came out silent and brick-heavy.

>   When the driver
finally dropped
us off, we emerged
dazed, clinging to one another for dear life.

A Very Old Story

Your great grandma
told the story
of when I was

three years old
and fell down the
basement stairs

with my tricycle.
She heard the
ruckus and arrived

to see me pick
myself up
and right the tricycle.

Before you ever fell
I had planned to tell you
do it with grace.

And then
stand up with pride.

The Role of the Poet

Aristotle said
the role of the poet
is not to ask

did it happen
but to imagine
could it happen

like strawberries
in the luscious of June
landing on

on cereal and milk,
sleepy palettes.

So many mornings
I had planned

to break
fast with you.

And many
mornings
I still do.

A Plea to You in Heaven

            haul the all
of the sky
down here

            and
stand still
let the bright

            shine
its light on
Mama, Daddy, Oma, Opa

            a latticework
of love adoring you
now and forever

How Long the Sad

it gets better, they say
time moves on, they say
keep busy, they say

live your life, they say
let go, they say
make a new story, they say

I try
yet every story
has a back-story

not to believe

Morning

every day I wake up
with a fresh case of missing

death can do that
set up a turn key

that cannot unlock

while I search for you
eyelids low with longing

if I experience a trauma
over which I have no control

I circle the post
from the past to the present

in the morning
in the evening

you know where you are
and I—I am dreaming

The Demonstration

I recall how
your mother taught you kindness
and you showed it
at day care

       with another
       toddler
       crabby and crying.

You scurried over
on all fours
a crawling machine
of comfort.

Upon reaching him
you pushed yourself
up, handed him his pacifier

and sat with him
as if to say
I know, I know.

The Velocity of Love

In the wishes of my kitchen
In the kitchen of my wish
            I yearn to feed you

To see you
            gum baby Mum Mums
            pinch the peas, loop
            fat fingers around green beans

I long to give you
            another Reliance peach, sticky ooze,
            lips like a reed making
            music with every um-mmmm mouthful

At Festival Foods,
            a toddler bright-eyed as an orange
            spies me, smiles—at me

Everywhere
I feel you: my head wobbly,
ribs imprisoned, heart seizing
at the thought of you
savoring, giggling, touching

My littlest love
who grew
to be
my largest

This, I Believe, Is What You Are Telling Me

Get a view.
Preferably a long one.
Short can work too.
Roar.
Growl if need be.
Judge no one.
Heat up.
Cool down.
Light a candle.
Listen to the body.
Favor circles over straight lines.
Wash your hands.
Check your pulse and then thank it.
Paddle through gossip.
Make big splashes.
Skip often.
Anoint your feet.
Mind the stars.
Mend torn thoughts.
Avoid compartments.
Be wrong.
Come closer.
Seek solitude.
Crack your back.
Expect the unknown.
Love with ease.
Laugh a lot.
Do not lean.
Be beautiful.
Be fierce.
Be anything but mad.

And then . . .

it is the Harvest Moon
except the sky stumbles in clouds.

No luminosity. Something makes me
stand and gaze,
                lost, transfixed by jagged dark.

                And then . . . an opening . . .
lacy clouds move
the moon into full face, your face—

cocoa eyes and fat glad cheeks
that vast smile of yours
spilling over
the
fractures
of my heart

the fissures

to let in dark
and bend it light

The Notion of Family, Now

Some families get along.
Some families leave it alone.
Some families crack and split.

But all families

whether
separately or together
find wrinkled hands
or sagging spines

that hang on

to age-old
desire
that can
never be

and yet
will
always
be.

Hope

In our time
period
we have produced
many know-it-alls

people
of all colors
ages, genders, and stages

doodle-brained and lame
stubborn to proselytize,
preach, and pontificate

except for you
a living mystery
I hope to intuit

every veiled truth
an upturn of your lips
intention in a gaze

of my sage, my old soul
tugging at me with divine grace
magnetic, downright electrifying

Beatitude (a state of utmost bliss)

What it took
to love flowed with
milk of human kindness

cheeks soft and giving
the grotto of a throat
hushed, lush.

I hear the mourning doves
though it is dusk

and feel you wrapped
around me

like a promise
to never leave

the way an echo
will not leave

and can be heard
long after gone

Birthday

on your next
birthday
on your every
birthday
I will celebrate
I will sing
loud and long
I will shout
   call out
I will keep going
until
the frog in my throat
turns
into a prince
and we
walk
the kingdom
you rule

As noon cruises toward afternoon

We come upon
the tepee

a species of idea
where we crawl in

drop the flap
and sit cross-legged

breathing
the depth of being

an eternal peace
you came from

and the one
you returned to

Last Night

Fireflies.
Fat stars.
The sky unlined.

And
pouring into
my hands

like moonlight—
you.

For Every Problem There is a Solution

many have gone
to bed flattened
tossed and tangled
all night

trembling the rafters
shivering the dreams

yet in the morning
a bluebird
who knows not
loneliness
lands

on the peach tree
in thin sunlight
flutters his tail

and flies away

How Much Light Is Too Much

the nth degree squared
the pi in your eye
a summer squash split

laughter as lucidity
belly of a high white cloud
a stained glass window glowing

your head on my chest
my heart in your hands
the small of me in the arc of you

a charged moment
sparkle and sizzle
on gratitude's whistle

to have seen you makes my life a remarkable one

it appears to be
a dream
state
in colors
of rain
beyond an indigo
sky
   your eyes
with hints of
why
when
   I reach for
you
and
you come
   to life

This Much I Know About Sorrow

Invisible, up till now

      as it is a force to inform
      beginning with
      solar storms that circle the sun

keeping the earth in orbit
a draw on the moon

how wind will heap dust
and thunder thrash memory

And so, I stand in this storm
lifting my face
sans umbrella
unafraid of

raging water
watery rage

Every feeling
I can feel
I will/I shall/I can/I must

In pounding dread
I feel for me
I feel for you—

my knight
whose sword
disturbs the piled up ash

because I will never
stop missing
every speck of you.

Blueprint

I once made a
life of eating and
dream-sleeping

dancing past the
night of mid-life

rearranging, erasing,
trying on roles
like skirts or shoes

writing a new script
drafting an arena
safe enough

to step into
the blueprint of who
I was meant to be

and you
the who
to follow.

But things change.

The House of Imagination

to
all
who
are broken
what
can
you
do
but
plant
a
seed
and
believe

In Search

> *What many have sought but failed to find,*
> *a few, by chance, have stumbled upon .*
>   - A. G. Lamb

and the ages
tell the tale

while the tale
carries the age

it is in wavering that
we learn to find balance

how we hold our
head to joy
because we have seen
another side

The universe is under no obligation to explain itself

Some say
you
are
a star

How can
they
say
that

when you
could
very well
be
a meteor

your own galaxy

You could be
the wide open wild
firmament itself

You could
You are

The Air There

the air there:
champagne,
quite beautified

my cheek against yours
a kiss chocolate or caramel
with a whiff of anise

in any case
smell the intergalactic lilacs
pick them
put them in a see-through vase

I will be there soon

Notes & Acknowledgements

These love notes were written in real time: before, during—and then, after—my grandson's life, not knowing how short a life it would be.

I am thankful for family and friends who sustained me. First and foremost, for my daughter Nora Zylstra, the reverse gear in her head, for my son Owen Zylstra, the smartest heart on the planet, for my brother Jon Freis, hand on my shoulder as I fielded phone calls/emails, and for my sister Mary Ann Schnur, who knew what to say and when. Grateful to my sister Lisa Vanden Avond and her son, Joe Vanden Avond for his exemplary empathy.

Heartfelt thanks to Bob and Holly Johnson circling me with age-old wisdom and grace. Thank you, Dianne Parisi, for showing up at my door with a red Talbots blazer, wrapping me with care every time I wear it. To Ellen O'Brien for faithful daily contact, illumination from a woman wounded and rising.

Deepest gratitude to Valerie Krejcie for unwavering attention and for taking me away on the California Zephyr when I needed perspective, distance. Special praise to Cheryl Bornemann, best cousin and librarian extraordinaire. High regard for women warriors like Ann Allen, erudite stagehand in the theater of the mind, Joyce Atkins decoding family history, Laurie Crawford coaching me toward authenticity, and Sharon Reilly opening her mouth like a bird to heal me.

And of course, indebtedness to writers who journeyed with me, including Mira Bartok, Jean Biegun, Sylvia Cavanaugh, Georgia Ressmeyer, Dawn Hogue, Blair Deets, Sandra Hurtes, Sarah Sadie, Lisa Vihos, Karl Elder, and Tara Pohlkotte, plus Michael Lucey, Jennifer Pody Gaskell, Amy Mazzarillo, and countless other friends.

And finally, to my beloved Leo. Thank you for coming.

Also by Kathryn Gahl

Life Drawing Class (2009)

"The graceful poems in Kathryn Gahl's collection titled LIFE DRAWING CLASS are an undeniable pleasure to read. Skillfully crafted, they reveal a firm control of pace, color and tone, taking the reader on an impressionistic journey through a high-risk world—from the poet's girlhood to her coming-of-age in uneasy times, through marriage, motherhood, bereavement—and finally coming to rest at a point in mid-life marked not only by grief and loss, but also by life-affirming gain and enlightenment. The elements that Gahl consciously borrows from the visual arts—line, shape, shadow and light—are all realized here with delicacy and considerable passion, 'recalling love/left in the marrow.'"

—Marilyn L. Taylor, former Wisconsin Poet Laureate

"Art, even poetry, has its stars and character actors, both of whom essentially mirror themselves. However, there is no type-casting Kathryn Gahl, as LIFE DRAWING CLASS, this, her first collection, attests, with no two poems quite alike, each having assumed the mantle of truth for the moment. Readers familiar with Walter Pater's 'To burn always with this hard, gemlike flame, to maintain this ecstasy, is success in life' will discover a kindred spirit here, the difference being never in the degree of energy the poet projects but in the many roles she assumes from sometimes sassy farm girl to savvy and sophisticated sensibility."

—Karl Elder, author of _Gilgamesh at the Bellagio_

available at
kathryngahl.com

Made in the USA
Monee, IL
29 September 2021

79011060R00066